Written by: Pamela Amick Klawitter, EdD
Editor: Regina Kim
Designer/Production: Rebekah O. Lewis
Cover Illustrator: Karl Edwards
Cover Designer: Barbara Peterson
Art Director: Moonhee Pak
Project Director: Stacey Faulkner

Table of Contents

Introduction

More I'm Through! What Can I Do? is a one-stop resource that addresses this all-too-familiar question teachers hear from students who finish early. The high-interest, ready-to-use puzzles, riddles, brainteasers, and mazes can be completed with minimal teacher assistance and help sharpen language arts, math, creative thinking, and critical thinking skills. This new series is a follow-up to our best-selling titles *I'm Through! What Can I Do?*

GETTING STARTED

Use any of the following suggestions to create a simple, structured environment that allows students to access these activities independently and keeps busy classrooms running smoothly.

1. Create individual student packets using all of the activity pages. Have students keep the packets in their desks and complete pages if they finish their assigned work early.

2. Create smaller packets by content areas (language arts and math) to use at centers. Store each set of packets in a file folder. Attach a class list to the outside of each folder. Have students cross out their names after they complete the packet.

3. Use activity pages individually as

- supplements to specific lessons
- homework assignments
- substitute teacher's helpers
- three-minute transition activities
- morning warm-up or after-lunch refocusing activities

HELPFUL TIPS TO FREE YOUR TIME

- Allow students to consult classmates to figure out puzzles.
- Encourage students to correct each other's work.
- Place copies of the answer key in an accessible area for students to pull as needed for self-correction.
- Give students copies of the Student Recording Sheet (page 4) to keep track of completed activity pages. Have students color in or check off each activity after it is completed.

However you choose to use the activity pages, let *More I'm Through! What Can I Do?* assist you in establishing a constructive and productive classroom environment.

Name: _____

Keep track of your work by filling in the box after completing the activity.

p. 5	p. 6	p. 7	p. 8	p. 9	p. 10	p. 11	p. 12	p. 13	p. 14
p. 15	p. 16	p. 17	p. 18	p. 19	p. 20	p. 21	p. 22	p. 23	p. 24
p. 25	p. 26	p. 27	p. 28	p. 29	p. 30	p. 31	p. 32	p. 33	p. 34
p. 35	p. 36	p. 37	p. 38	p. 39	p. 40	p. 41	p. 42	p. 43	p. 44
p. 45	p. 46	p. 47	p. 48	p. 49	p. 50	p. 51	p. 52	p. 53	p. 54
p. 55	p. 56	p. 57	p. 58	p. 59	p. 60	p. 61	p. 62	p. 63	p. 64
p. 65	p. 66	p. 67	p. 68	p. 69	p. 70	p. 71	p. 72	p. 73	p. 74
p. 75	p. 76	p. 77	p. 78	p. 79	p. 80	p. 81	p. 82	p. 83	p. 84
p. 85	p. 86	p. 87	p. 88	p. 89	p. 90				

Word Maker #1

How many words can you find in the Word Maker square? There are more than 50 words! Start your list below. Then challenge a friend to see who can find the most words.

Rules to remember:

- The words you find must have 3 or more letters.
- From any beginning letter, build a word by going left, right, up, down, or diagonally. (A single word may go in more than one direction.)
- You may not skip a square. Each letter in a word must touch the squares before and after it.
- The same letter square can be used more than once in a word, but it cannot be used twice in a row.
- The star can count for any letter, and it can be used twice in a row.
- Proper nouns (e.g., *Harry*) are not allowed.

a	s	t	o
n	★	e	l
p	i	r	m
l	a	c	t

_____   _____   _____

_____   _____   _____

_____   _____   _____

_____   _____   _____

_____   _____   _____

Word Maker #2

How many words can you find in the Word Maker square? There are more than 50 words! Start your list below. Then challenge a friend to see who can find the most words.

Rules to remember:

- The words you find must have 3 or more letters.
- From any beginning letter, build a word by going left, right, up, down, or diagonally. (A single word may go in more than one direction.)
- You may not skip a square. Each letter in a word must touch the squares before and after it.
- The same letter square can be used more than once in a word, but it cannot be used twice in a row.
- The star can count for any letter, and it can be used twice in a row.
- Proper nouns (e.g., *Harry*) are not allowed.

e	r	p	a
d	n	t	s
i	★	c	o
w	u	b	e

_____   _____   _____

_____   _____   _____

_____   _____   _____

_____   _____   _____

_____   _____   _____

More I'm Through! What Can I Do? Grade 5 © 2008 Creative Teaching Press

Word Maker #3

How many words can you find in the Word Maker square? There are more than 50 words! Start your list below. Then challenge a friend to see who can find the most words.

Rules to remember:

- The words you find must have 3 or more letters.
- From any beginning letter, build a word by going left, right, up, down, or diagonally. (A single word may go in more than one direction.)
- You may not skip a square. Each letter in a word must touch the squares before and after it.
- The same letter square can be used more than once in a word, but it cannot be used twice in a row.
- The star can count for any letter, and it can be used twice in a row.
- Proper nouns (e.g., *Harry*) are not allowed.

e	t	a	s	r
n	r	o	e	i
m	a	t	★	w
c	y	d	i	n
e	f	a	h	p

_____   _____   _____

_____   _____   _____

_____   _____   _____

_____   _____   _____

_____   _____   _____

More I'm Through! What Can I Do? Grade 5 © 2008 Creative Teaching Press

Word Maker #4

How many words can you find in the Word Maker square? There are more than 50 words! Start your list below. Then challenge a friend to see who can find the most words.

Rules to remember:

- The words you find must have 3 or more letters.
- From any beginning letter, build a word by going left, right, up, down, or diagonally. (A single word may go in more than one direction.)
- You may not skip a square. Each letter in a word must touch the squares before and after it.
- The same letter square can be used more than once in a word, but it cannot be used twice in a row.
- The star can count for any letter, and it can be used twice in a row.
- Proper nouns (e.g., *Harry*) are not allowed.

t	r	i	k	n
a	l	e	s	u
g	n	b	i	c
e	r	★	t	n
l	f	y	o	p

_____   _____   _____

_____   _____   _____

_____   _____   _____

_____   _____   _____

_____   _____   _____

More I'm Through! What Can I Do? Grade 5 © 2008 Creative Teaching Press

Triplets

Think fast! Try to find **20** three-letter words using only the letters on the tiles below. No proper nouns!
A letter may only be used once per word.

Examples: bar, rib, aim

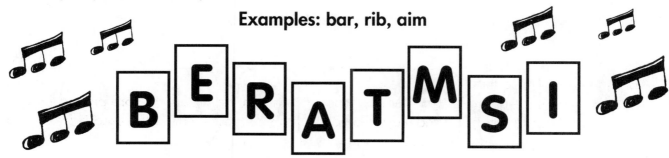

1. _____

2. _____

3. _____

4. _____

5. _____

6. _____

7. _____

8. _____

9. _____

10. _____

11. _____

12. _____

13. _____

14. _____

15. _____

16. _____

17. _____

18. _____

19. _____

20. _____

More I'm Through! What Can I Do? Grade 5 © 2008 Creative Teaching Press

Name: ______________________________ Date: ______________

Juggling Vowels

Make 3 words in each row by adding 3 different pairs of vowels between the beginning and ending consonants shown. The same vowel **may** be used more than once per word.

Examples: b __ __ t ⟶ beat, beet, boot, boat, bout

A E I O U

s__ __l	s__ __l	s__ __l
f__ __l	f__ __l	f__ __l
l__ __n	l__ __n	l__ __n
p__ __r	p__ __r	p__ __r
m__ __n	m__ __n	m__ __n
d__ __d	d__ __d	d__ __d
t__ __r	t__ __r	t__ __r

More I'm Through! What Can I Do? Grade 5 © 2008 Creative Teaching Press

Name: _____   Date: _____

Rhyme Time

Find **10** pairs of five-letter rhyming words using only the letters in the gears below. A letter **may** be used more than once per word. A word may not be used in more than one pair. No proper nouns!

Example: notes & moats

e o a s m r t n h d

1. _____ _____ _____ _____ _____ & _____ _____ _____ _____ _____
2. _____ _____ _____ _____ _____ & _____ _____ _____ _____ _____
3. _____ _____ _____ _____ _____ & _____ _____ _____ _____ _____
4. _____ _____ _____ _____ _____ & _____ _____ _____ _____ _____
5. _____ _____ _____ _____ _____ & _____ _____ _____ _____ _____
6. _____ _____ _____ _____ _____ & _____ _____ _____ _____ _____
7. _____ _____ _____ _____ _____ & _____ _____ _____ _____ _____
8. _____ _____ _____ _____ _____ & _____ _____ _____ _____ _____
9. _____ _____ _____ _____ _____ & _____ _____ _____ _____ _____
10. _____ _____ _____ _____ _____ & _____ _____ _____ _____ _____

More I'm Through! What Can I Do? Grade 5 © 2008 Creative Teaching Press

Fill 'er Up

Fill each box with words that begin and end as shown on the top of the box.
Words must be at least five letters long. No proper nouns!

Examples: b ____ r ➞ barter, binder, briar, boulder, bachelor, bricklayer

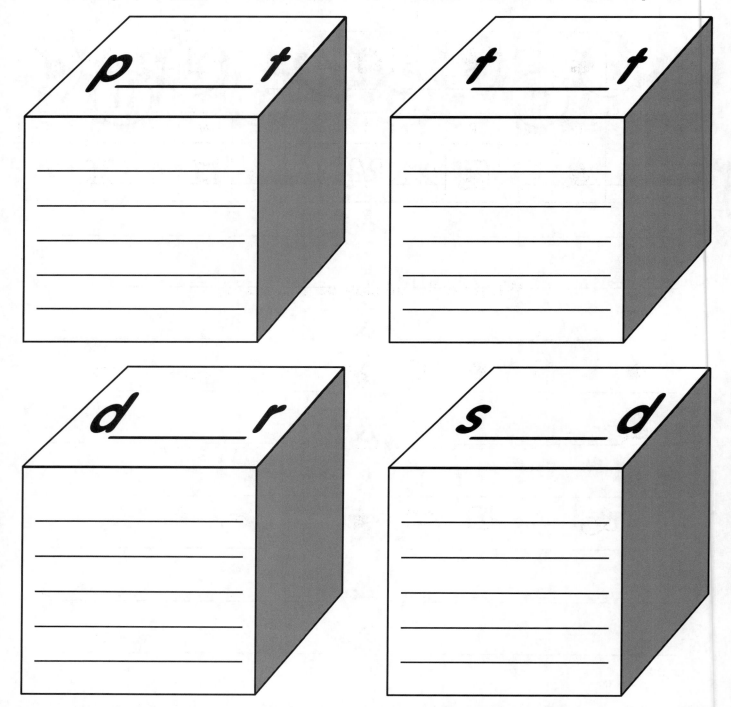

Code Breaker #1

Find the answer to the riddle by writing a letter for each picture symbol on the lines below. The first letter has been done for you.

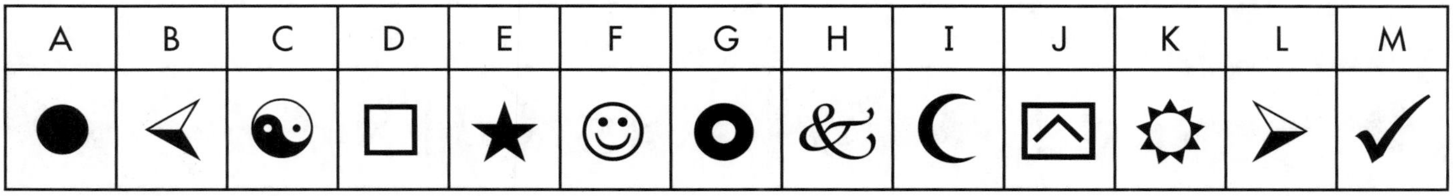

A	B	C	D	E	F	G	H	I	J	K	L	M
●	◄	☯	□	★	☺	◉	&	☾	⌂	☼	➤	✓

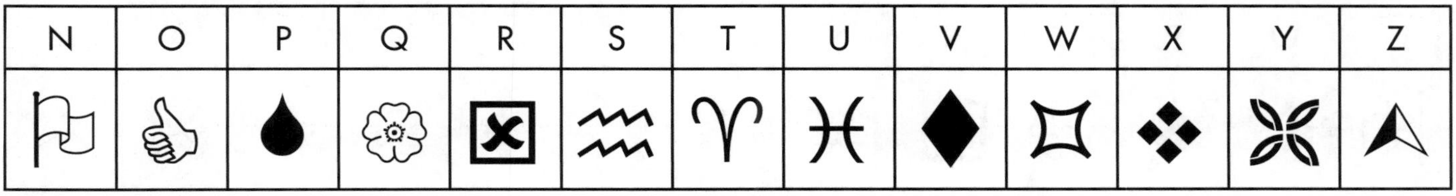

N	O	P	Q	R	S	T	U	V	W	X	Y	Z
⚑	👍	●	✿	⊠	≈	♈	♓	◆	◇	❖	❋	◄

What walks all day on its head?

● ⚑ ● ☾ ➤   ☾ ⚑   ●

A_ _ _ _ _   _ _   _

& 👍 ⊠ ≈ ★ ≈ & 👍 ★

_ _ _ _ _ _ _ _ _ .

Name: _____   Date: _____

Code Breaker #2

Find the answer to the riddle by writing a letter for each picture symbol on the lines below. The first letter has been done for you.

A	B	C	D	E	F	G	H	I	J	K	L	M
●	◄	☯	□	★	☺	◉	&	☾	⌂	✿	➤	✓

N	O	P	Q	R	S	T	U	V	W	X	Y	Z
⚑	👍	💧	✽	⊠	≋	♈	♓	◆	◇	❖	✵	➤

Why do birds fly south?

B _ _ _ _ _ _ _ _ _

_ _ _ _ _ _ _ _ _ _

_ _ _ _ _ _ _ .

More I'm Through! What Can I Do? Grade 5 © 2008 Creative Teaching Press

Code Breaker #3

Find the answer to the riddle by writing a letter for each picture symbol on the lines below. The first letter has been done for you.

A	B	C	D	E	F	G	H	I	J	K	L	M
●	◄	☯	□	★	☺	◉	&	☾	⌂	☀	➤	✓

N	O	P	Q	R	S	T	U	V	W	X	Y	Z
⚑	👍	💧	✿	⊠	〰	♈	♓	◆	✦	❖	✤	➤

What time is it when the elephant sits on the fence?

♈ C ✓ ★   ♈ 👍   ◉ ★ ♈

T _ _ _   _ _   _ _ _

●   ⚑ ★ ✦   ☺ ★ ⚑ ☯ ★

_   _ _ _ _   _ _ _ _ _ .

A Way with Words **15**

Name: _____   Date: _____

Skateboarding Fun

How many words can you make using the letters in **skateboarding fun**? Start your list on the lines below. Challenge a friend to beat your score!

Rules to remember:

- Each word must have at least 3 letters.
- Use only the letters you see in **skateboarding fun**.
- You may only use a letter as many times as it appears.
  For example, you may not have a word with 2 **e**'s because there is only 1 **e** in **skateboarding fun**.
- No proper nouns! (e.g., *Harry*).

Scoring:

Three-letter word	= 1 point
Four-letter word	= 2 points
Five-letter word	= 3 points
Six or more letters	= 4 points

_____ _____ _____

_____ _____ _____

_____ _____ _____

_____ _____ _____

_____ _____ _____

_____ _____ _____

_____ _____ _____

_____ _____ _____

Number of words I found: _____   **Points:** _____

More I'm Through! What Can I Do? Grade 5 © 2008 Creative Teaching Press

Name: _____   Date: _____

Rock Climbing Adventure

How many words can you make using the letters in **rock climbing adventure**? Start your list on the lines below. Challenge a friend to beat your score!

Rules to remember:

- Each word must have at least 3 letters.
- Use only the letters you see in **rock climbing adventure**.
- You may only use a letter as many times as it appears. For example, you may not have a word with 2 **a**'s because there is only 1 **a** in **rock climbing adventure**.
- No proper nouns! (e.g., *Harry*).

Scoring:

Three-letter word   = 1 point
Four-letter word   = 2 points
Five-letter word   = 3 points
Six or more letters   = 4 points

_____ _____ _____

_____ _____ _____

_____ _____ _____

_____ _____ _____

_____ _____ _____

_____ _____ _____

_____ _____ _____

_____ _____ _____

Number of words I found: _____   **Points:** _____

More I'm Through! What Can I Do? Grade 5 © 2008 Creative Teaching Press

Name: _____ Date: _____

State Stumper Crossword

Read each clue. Find the state name that correctly answers each clue. Write the answer in the puzzle grid. You may look at a U.S. map for help.

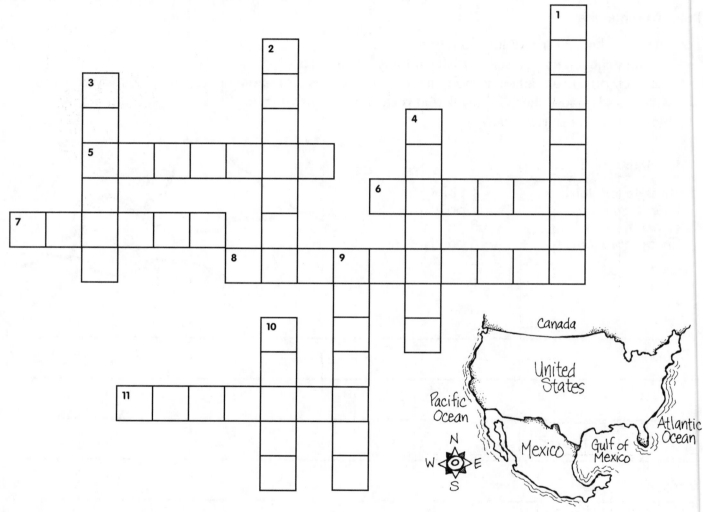

Across

5. I'm the only state that touches both Lake Erie and Lake Ontario.
6. I touch both Idaho and Nevada.
7. I am closer to Asia than any other state.
8. I touch both Mexico and the Pacific Ocean.
11. I am closer to Cuba than any other state.

Down

1. I touch both Kentucky and the Atlantic Ocean.
2. I am between South Carolina and Alabama.
3. I touch both Colorado and Nebraska, but not South Dakota.
4. I touch both Canada and Massachusetts, but not Maine.
9. I touch both Lake Michigan and Kentucky.
10. I touch Canada and only one state.

More I'm Through! What Can I Do? Grade 5 © 2008 Creative Teaching Press

Spelling Stumper Crossword

Read each clue. Find the word that is spelled incorrectly in each sentence. Write the correctly spelled word in the puzzle grid.

giraffe?

girafe?

Across

3. The budderflie landed on my nose!
5. Did you know that a schrimp has ten legs?
8. One type of raddlesnake is the diamondback.
10. A donky is often very stubborn.
11. A dragenfly is sometimes called a darning needle.

Down

1. A gerble is a very popular pet.
2. An elafant is the largest land animal alive today.
3. A buffaloe has long shaggy hair.
4. A parrakete mostly eats seeds and fruit.
6. A hampster can carry lots of food in its cheek pouches.
7. A camal is often used to carry heavy loads across the desert.
9. A male turckey is called a tom and a female is called a hen.

Name: _____   Date: _____

Weather Word Search

The words listed below are in the puzzle horizontally, vertically, and diagonally. Can you find all of them? Circle or lightly shade the words as you find them.

hurricane	hail	squall
tornado	wind	frost
snow	lightning	dew
typhoon	thunder	monsoon
rain	heat wave	fog
drought	flood	
sleet	blizzard	

W	E	A	R	T	E	H	R	T	H	U	S	Q	S	U	I	Z	F	O	T
O	T	S	O	R	F	F	L	I	E	R	S	U	N	A	B	I	S	T	D
N	O	M	O	S	O	R	L	O	O	U	T	Q	O	F	L	C	A	R	R
L	I	H	N	T	G	O	Y	M	B	D	N	I	W	C	L	A	W	E	O
R	A	I	L	F	I	B	L	I	Z	S	N	O	Q	U	A	T	S	U	U
N	A	I	N	B	M	I	T	O	R	Z	Z	D	R	O	U	L	L	C	G
R	A	I	V	L	E	R	N	O	O	S	N	O	M	U	Q	L	H	A	H
H	U	R	R	I	C	A	N	E	C	M	O	N	S	O	S	L	E	E	T
M	O	O	P	Z	L	A	S	O	T	J	Y	G	I	L	Q	T	A	U	C
E	N	T	E	Z	R	T	A	I	O	N	M	E	L	N	U	T	T	O
N	C	L	C	A	M	I	T	O	R	H	A	F	I	O	P	W	W	E	E
I	O	A	K	R	T	D	U	A	L	L	P	N	G	C	S	R	A	L	F
O	I	U	L	D	E	E	L	L	O	I	N	Y	H	I	Z	E	V	U	I
P	N	Q	M	O	N	L	O	D	A	N	R	O	T	A	T	Z	E	V	W
E	Y	U	O	N	H	W	A	O	Z	Z	R	I	N	R	E	T	O	P	E
R	T	Z	I	E	G	P	W	O	L	B	B	M	I	E	D	E	T	Y	D
W	R	A	P	A	P	V	E	L	F	R	E	D	N	U	H	T	C	F	R
A	R	I	E	L	Z	E	S	F	O	R	T	N	G	R	E	E	T	Y	M
S	C	L	E	A	N	M	E	R	C	T	B	W	X	Q	U	I	O	P	Z
Q	U	A	L	T	Y	E	R	W	D	E	I	O	P	L	R	A	I	H	N

More I'm Through! What Can I Do? Grade 5 © 2008 Creative Teaching Press

Get a Job Word Search

The words listed below are in the puzzle horizontally, vertically, and diagonally. Can you find all of them? Circle or lightly shade the words as you find them.

doctor	mechanic	artist
plumber	reporter	pilot
actor	writer	astronaut
teacher	dancer	nurse
electrician	engineer	archaeologist
politician	lawyer	technician
model	architect	photographer
carpenter	judge	landscaper

P	L	A	N	D	A	R	C	H	P	O	L	R	E	T	R	O	P	E	R
O	S	O	L	D	A	S	T	R	O	N	A	U	T	A	S	T	L	I	N
L	O	T	E	C	H	N	I	C	I	A	N	M	E	N	C	V	H	I	E
I	X	E	R	T	Y	L	C	R	U	I	G	H	S	T	R	E	E	S	W
T	E	A	T	L	A	W	Y	E	R	W	E	Y	R	P	U	M	N	B	E
I	C	T	R	W	C	A	T	O	R	E	B	M	U	L	P	X	E	O	P
C	E	Y	E	E	M	S	P	T	O	D	O	C	N	T	Y	R	N	L	O
I	U	U	L	A	I	T	U	I	T	E	J	Q	U	E	A	S	A	T	G
A	I	H	P	T	N	G	H	U	C	R	U	M	E	R	E	T	I	R	W
N	P	J	R	H	T	D	O	C	O	X	D	Z	E	R	O	I	C	E	E
H	L	A	E	E	S	M	E	T	D	L	G	A	S	U	M	C	I	H	A
I	A	C	P	F	L	S	C	A	N	A	E	M	I	E	C	K	R	P	T
U	R	E	A	T	E	A	C	H	E	R	K	K	C	L	A	I	T	A	Y
K	E	R	C	C	D	W	L	O	V	S	A	H	R	A	H	P	C	R	B
L	E	T	S	W	O	I	J	S	E	I	A	W	A	L	M	E	E	G	E
O	N	U	D	O	M	T	T	E	R	N	T	T	E	K	I	R	L	O	P
B	I	I	N	L	A	R	C	H	I	T	E	C	T	E	C	S	E	T	I
R	G	A	A	I	N	H	O	C	K	R	A	M	E	L	H	T	P	O	L
E	N	S	L	P	R	E	T	N	E	P	R	A	C	L	E	E	A	H	O
N	E	Q	U	E	T	S	I	G	O	L	O	E	A	H	C	R	A	P	T

Word Chain #1

How long can you make each word chain? Continue each chain until you can't add another word. Look at the example, and follow the rules below.

Rules to remember:

- Begin with the words shown in each box.
- Follow the rule shown in the box.
- Add as many words as possible.
- You may not use a word more than once.
- No proper nouns (e.g., *John*).

Example: Each word in the chain must have two letters and begin with the last letter of the previous word. ➡ *oh, hi, it, to, on, no, or*

1. Each word in the chain must have three letters and begin with the last letter of the previous word.➡ **bat, toe,** _____

   _____

   _____

2. Each word in the chain must have one more letter than the previous word and begin with the same letter each time. ➡ **to, tie,**_____

   _____

   _____

3. Each word in the chain must begin with the last two letters of the previous word. ➡ **wasp,**

   spade, _____

   _____

   _____

More I'm Through! What Can I Do? Grade 5 © 2008 Creative Teaching Press

Word Chain #2

How long can you make each word chain? Continue each chain until you can't add another word. Look at the example, and follow the rules below.

Rules to remember:

- Begin with the words shown in each box.
- Follow the rule shown in the box.
- Add as many words as possible.
- You may not use a word more than once.
- No proper nouns (e.g., *John*).

Example: Each word in the chain must have two letters and begin with the last letter of the previous word. ⟶ *oh, hi, it, to, on, no, or*

---

1. Each word in the chain must begin with the same two letters as the previous word and must have five letters. ⟶ **spell, spicy,** _____

_____

_____

---

2. Each word in the chain must have five letters and begin with the last letter of the previous word.

⟶ **parks, scram,** _____

_____

_____

---

3. Each word in the chain must begin with the same letter as the previous word and have one less letter. ⟶ **steamboats, shoveling,** _____

_____

_____

Addition Pathways

Begin with the "start" number. Move vertically or horizontally through the maze, one square at a time. Use addition to reach the "finish" number at the end of the path. Draw a line to show your path. No square may be used more than once, and some squares won't be used at all. You must end with the total in the "finish" box.

START 1	10	11	5	23	
	6	19	16	9	
	28	5	40	17	
	15	12	14	8	105 FINISH

START 2	8	9	6	11	
	12	19	17	5	
	3	13	21	18	
	22	10	16	14	89 FINISH

START 5	6	11	22	12	
	17	15	9	33	
	27	3	18	7	
	21	31	4	8	101 FINISH

More I'm Through! What Can I Do? Grade 5 © 2008 Creative Teaching Press

Subtraction Pathways

Begin with the "start" number. Move vertically or horizontally through the maze, one square at a time. Use subtraction to reach the "finish" number at the end of the path. Draw a line to show your path. No square may be used more than once, and some squares won't be used at all. You must end with the total in the "finish" box.

START 100	24	4	14	7	
	16	2	18	22	
	31	17	12	9	
	10	6	15	13	1 FINISH

START 99	8	7	29	16	
	20	21	15	30	
	12	13	6	14	
	29	11	10	4	5 FINISH

START 101	3	5	14	6	
	27	33	21	9	
	17	22	16	15	
	19	31	10	13	2 FINISH

What's the Sum?

Begin each problem at the ★ square. Follow the directions and write down the number where you land. At the end of each pair of directions, add and write the sum on the line. The first number is shown.

200		603				700		299
	222			399			888	
333	187		666		709			400
	545	389		650		902		377
799		800		★	119		444	
	180		775		599			600
		199		356		175		209
188	207				215			898
		654		105			295	

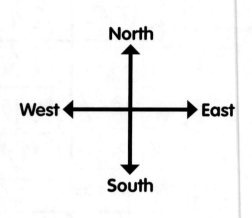

(1) N4, E4, S2 = __**400**__

S3, E1, N3 = _____

Add ➞ _____

(2) N3, W4, S1 = _____

W4, S2, E2 = _____

Add ➞ _____

(3) N2, S6, N2 = _____

E2, S3, W5 = _____

Add ➞ _____

(4) S1, E2, N5 = _____

N3, E3, S3 = _____

Add ➞ _____

(5) S1, E2, N2 = _____

W4, S1, E5 = _____

Add ➞ _____

(6) N2, W1, S3 = _____

S2, E4, N3 = _____

Add ➞ _____

(7) S3, W2, S1 = _____

E4, N1, W6 = _____

Add ➞ _____

(8) N3, W2, N1 = _____

W4, S2, E2 = _____

Add ➞ _____

More I'm Through! What Can I Do? Grade 5 © 2008 Creative Teaching Press

What's the Difference?

Begin each problem at the ★ square. Follow the directions and write down the number where you land. At the end of each pair of directions, subtract and write the difference on the line. The first number is shown.

	222		255		799		500		826	
199	200	111	716	355	464	469	399	595	666	681
	333	299	300	792	343	155	400	262	197	
364	955	557	699	900	★	444	777	894	499	547
	897	375	179	253	600	287	700	369	899	
695	756	800	359	289	884	599	349	852	357	278
	567		391		429		286		672	

North
West ← → **East**
South

(1) N2, E2, S3 = __**700**__

W1, S1, E2 = _____

Subtract ➞ _____

(2) S2, E2, N4 = _____

W4, N2, E1 = _____

Subtract ➞ _____

(3) S2, W4, N4 = _____

N2, W2, S3 = _____

Subtract ➞ _____

(4) E1, N1, W3 = _____

S2, E1, N3 = _____

Subtract ➞ _____

(5) W4, S2, E1 = _____

N2, E4, S5 = _____

Subtract ➞ _____

(6) W1, S1, E1 = _____

N2, W3, S1 = _____

Subtract ➞ _____

(7) E4, N1, W2 = _____

S1, W4, N2 = _____

Subtract ➞ _____

(8) N2, W1, S2 = _____

S2, E4, N4 = _____

Subtract ➞ _____

Tricky Subtraction

Begin each problem at the ★ square. Follow the directions and write down the number where you land. At the end of each pair of directions, subtract and write the difference on the line. The first number is shown.

211		255		809		765		134
	888	198	765	432	107	265	333	
789	100	218	665	466	234	516	132	267
	879	211	877	657	455	344	290	
907	564	176	643	155	210	285	674	231
	787	554	409	964	153	271	299	
896	276	391	271	201	864	291	276	391
	777	865	110	899	123	301	651	
896		222		★		854		109

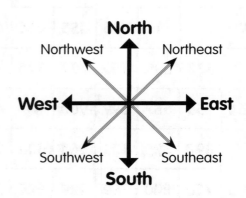

(1) NW3, NE2, W1 = _____ **211** _____

 N8, SW4, E2 = _____

 Subtract ➜ _____

(2) NE4, NW1, S1 = _____

 NW4, E8, NW3 = _____

 Subtract ➜ _____

(3) NE3, W4, SW3 = _____

 N5, SW2, E1 = _____

 Subtract ➜ _____

(4) NE3, N4, W4 = _____

 NW1, NE3, SE1 = _____

 Subtract ➜ _____

(5) NE1, NW3, S2 = _____

 N4, NE1, NW3 = _____

 Subtract ➜ _____

(6) NW3, E3, SE2 = _____

 N5, E3, SW2 = _____

 Subtract ➜ _____

(7) NW3, E4, S1 = _____

 NE4, W5, NW1 = _____

 Subtract ➜ _____

(8) N6, SE3, W3 = _____

 NW4, NE3, SE1 = _____

 Subtract ➜ _____

More I'm Through! What Can I Do? Grade 5 © 2008 Creative Teaching Press

Math Mysteries

Begin each problem at the ★ square. Follow the directions carefully. The first set of directions in each problem will show you which operation to use. The remaining two sets of directions will show you which two numbers to use in solving the problem.

				155				
			505	368	609			
		192	327	975	÷	188		
77	42	80	16	40	98	35	30	10
143	x	451	966	112	758	853	120	386
722	843	795	124	907	488	659	—	700
+	20	13	54	★	86	17	44	52

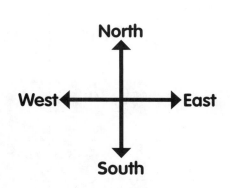

(1) N3, E3, S2 = + − x ÷

W2, N4, E2 = _____

E2, N2, E2 = _____

Answer ⟶ _____

(2) N3, W4, S3 = + − x ÷

N3, W3, S2 = _____

N2, E2, S1 = _____

Answer ⟶ _____

(3) E1, N2, W4 = + − x ÷

E1, N2, W2 = _____

W2, N3, E2 = _____

Answer ⟶ _____

(4) W2, N4, E3 = + − x ÷

E2, N4, W2 = _____

N2, W2, S2 = _____

Answer ⟶ _____

(5) N2, W4, S2 = + − x ÷

W2, N4, E4 = _____

N4, W1, S2 = _____

Answer ⟶ _____

(6) E1, N2, W4 = + − x ÷

E2, N3, E1 = _____

N2, W1, S2 = _____

Answer ⟶ _____

Math Path #1

Begin with the number next to the "start." Continue through the maze by adding, subtracting, multiplying, and dividing until you come to the "end." Write your final answer in the circle.

Start	162	+	168	−
				125
				x
237	+	15	÷	3
−				
199				
x	12	+	165	End

More I'm Through! What Can I Do? Grade 5 © 2008 Creative Teaching Press

Math Path #2

Start with the "input" number for each problem. Decide if the number is prime or composite. Follow the appropriate arrows below and use the key to determine which operation to use to help you reach the output number.

Example: Input = 12. Since 12 is composite, complete the following steps to get an answer:

Input	= 12
12 x 27	= 324
324 + 499	= 823
823 – 555	= 268
Output	= 268

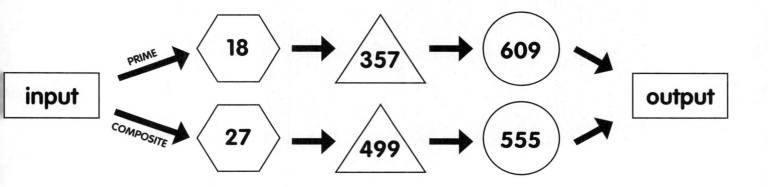

	Input	Output	Key
1.	29		⬡ = multiply
2.	48		
3.	67		△ = add
4.	72		
5.	95		◯ = subtract

Number Puzzle #1

Use the numbers and shapes in the Venn diagram below to answer each question.

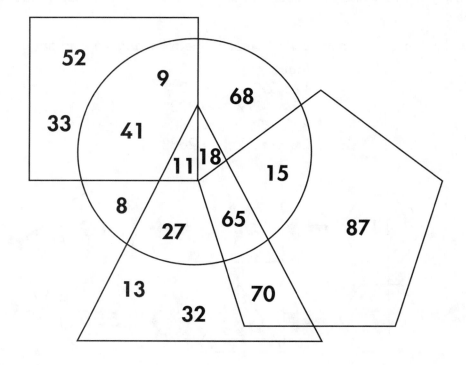

1. What is the sum of the numbers that are inside the circle, but not inside the pentagon? _____

2. What is the product of the two largest numbers that lie inside the circle? _____

3. What is the product of the two largest numbers that lie outside the circle? _____

4. What is the difference between the sum of all the numbers inside the circle and all the numbers inside the pentagon? _____

5. Which of the four large shapes has the smallest sum when all numbers inside its border are added? _____

   What is the sum? _____

6. What is the product of the largest even number in the square and the largest odd number in the pentagon? _____

More I'm Through! What Can I Do? Grade 5 © 2008 Creative Teaching Press

Number Puzzle #2

Each piece of candy in the rectangle contains chocolate. Each piece in the circle contains raisins. Each piece in the triangle contains peanuts. Use this information to answer the following questions.

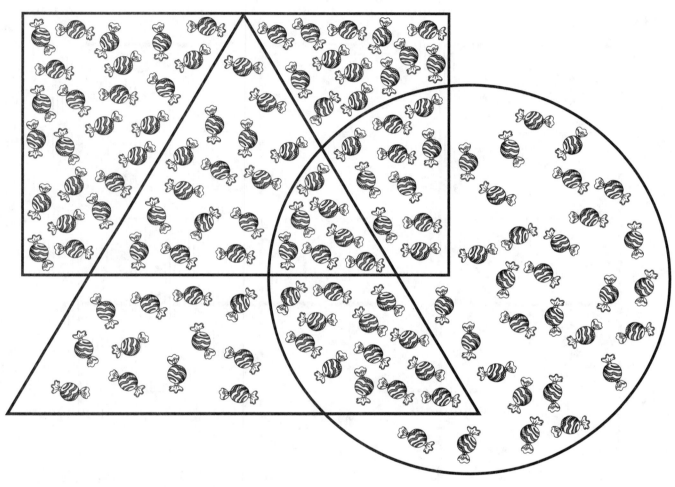

How many pieces of candy contain…

1. only chocolate? _____

2. only peanuts? _____

3. only raisins? _____

4. only peanuts and raisins? _____

5. only raisins and chocolate? _____

6. only peanuts and chocolate? _____

7. raisins, chocolate, and peanuts? _____

8. no peanuts? _____

9. no raisins? _____

10. no chocolate? _____

It All Adds Up #1

In this puzzle, there are 6 rows, 6 columns, and 6 mini-grids of 6 squares each. Using only the numbers 1 through 6, fill in the grid so that every row, every column, and every mini-grid of six squares contains the numbers 1 through 6. No number may be repeated within a column, row, or mini-grid.

5	1				6
		6	5	2	1
			1		5
4		1			
1	6	4	3		
2				1	4

More I'm Through! What Can I Do? Grade 5 © 2008 Creative Teaching Press

It All Adds Up #2

In this puzzle, there are 6 rows, 6 columns, and 6 mini-grids of 6 squares each. Using only the numbers 1 through 6, fill in the grid so that every row, every column, and every mini-grid of six squares contains the numbers 1 through 6. No number may be repeated within a column, row, or mini-grid.

	1	3	4		6
3				1	
	6		1		3
1		4		6	
	3				2
5		6	2	3	

More I'm Through! What Can I Do? Grade 5 © 2008 Creative Teaching Press

Name: _____   Date: _____

It All Adds Up #3

In this puzzle, there are 6 rows, 6 columns, and 6 mini-grids of 6 squares each. Using only the numbers 1 through 6, fill in the grid so that every row, every column, and every mini-grid of six squares, contains the numbers 1 through 6. No number may be repeated within a column, row, or mini-grid.

4		5	2	1	
5	1				4
	2		4		
		4		6	
6				3	5
	5	3	6		2

More I'm Through! What Can I Do? Grade 5 © 2008 Creative Teaching Press

It All Adds Up #4

In this puzzle, there are 6 rows, 6 columns, and 6 mini-grids of 6 squares each. Using only the numbers 1 through 6, fill in the grid so that every row, every column, and every mini-grid of six squares contains the numbers 1 through 6. No number may be repeated within a column, row, or mini-grid.

			1		6
1	6			3	2
5		2		4	
	4		2		3
3	1			2	5
2		1			

It All Adds Up #5

In this puzzle, there are 9 rows, 9 columns, and 9 mini-grids of 9 squares each. Using only the numbers 1 through 9, fill in the grid so that every row, every column, and every mini-grid of nine squares contains the numbers 1 through 9. No number may be repeated within a column, row, or mini-grid.

7					5	6		9
1		5		3	4		2	
		3	2		7			4
	4		6	7		9	1	
3	1						8	6
	9			1	3		7	
2			8		6	5		
			7	9		3		1
6		9	3					2

More I'm Through! What Can I Do? Grade 5 © 2008 Creative Teaching Press

It All Adds Up #6

In this puzzle, there are 9 rows, 9 columns, and 9 mini-grids of 9 squares each. Using only the numbers 1 through 9, fill in the grid so that every row, every column, and every mini-grid of nine squares contains the numbers 1 through 9. No number may be repeated within a column, row, or mini-grid.

			5		7			
7		8				9		5
	2	5				8	6	
	3			9			5	
	1	7	6		2	3	8	
	8			3			9	
	5	1				6	7	
4		9				2		1
			9		6			

It All Adds Up #7

In this puzzle, there are 9 rows, 9 columns, and 9 mini-grids of 9 squares each. Using only the numbers 1 through 9, fill in the grid so that every row, every column, and every mini-grid of nine squares contains the numbers 1 through 9. No number may be repeated within a column, row, or mini-grid.

	1	2		7		3	9	
6			5		3			8
5								4
	9			2			4	
			6		7			
	4			5			8	
4								2
9			1		2			7
	8	1		6		5	3	

More I'm Through! What Can I Do? Grade 5 © 2008 Creative Teaching Press

It All Adds Up #8

In this puzzle, there are 9 rows, 9 columns, and 9 mini-grids of 9 squares each. Using only the numbers 1 through 9, fill in the grid so that every row, every column, and every mini-grid of nine squares contains the numbers 1 through 9. No number may be repeated within a column, row, or mini-grid.

					1	7	8	9
4			3	7		6		2
1		2		9			5	
			5	8			3	
	1	6				8	4	
	3			4	6			
	6			5		9		4
5		8		6	7			1
3	9	7	2					

What a Pickle!

Choose digits from the pickles below to make the numbers required for each question. A digit may only be used once per number (for example, you may make 597 but not 997 because there is only one 9 shown). Be sure to show the number sentence you make to get the answer for each problem.

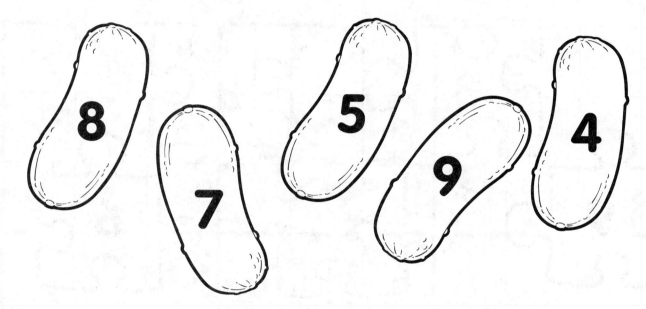

1. What is the difference between the largest and the smallest 3-digit numbers you can make?

   _____

2. What is the sum of the four largest 3-digit numbers you can make?

   _____

3. What is the difference between the largest even 3-digit number and the smallest odd 3-digit number you can make?

   _____

4. What is the sum of the five largest 2-digit numbers you can make?

   _____

5. What is the difference between the largest and smallest 4-digit numbers you can make?

   _____

More I'm Through! What Can I Do? Grade 5 © 2008 Creative Teaching Press

Name: _____   Date: _____

I'm Puzzled

Choose digits from the puzzle pieces below to make the numbers required for each question. A digit may only be used once per number (for example, you may make 497 but not 997 because there is only one 9 shown). Be sure to show the number sentence you make to get the answer for each problem.

1. What is the difference between the largest and the smallest 4-digit numbers you can make?

   _____

2. What is the sum of the four largest 4-digit numbers you can make?

   _____

3. What is the difference between the largest odd 4-digit number and the smallest even 4-digit number you can make?

   _____

4. What is the sum of the five largest 3-digit numbers you can make?

   _____

5. What is the difference between the largest and smallest 5-digit numbers you can make?

   _____

More I'm Through! What Can I Do? Grade 5 © 2008 Creative Teaching Press

B-I-N-G-O!

Use the *Bingo* card to answer the questions below.

	B	I	N	G	O	TOTAL
Row 1	3	20	41	60	63	_____
Row 2	8	16	39	55	75	_____
Row 3	12	30	FREE	48	66	_____
Row 4	7	28	42	59	68	_____
Row 5	15	19	33	47	71	_____

TOTAL   _____   _____   _____   _____   _____

Give the total for each row and column on the lines provided above, and then answer the following questions.

1. Find the difference between the totals for the highest and lowest rows.   _____

2. How much more does the column **O** total than row **5**?   _____

3. Find the difference between the totals for the highest and lowest columns.   _____

4. What number would need to be removed from column **G** to make the total 221?   _____

More I'm Through! What Can I Do? Grade 5 © 2008 Creative Teaching Press

Odd Word Out #1

In each row, all of the words have something in common except one. Find and circle the word that doesn't belong in each row.

1. flock   herd   bunch   pack   colony

2. big   huge   gigantic   large   minor

3. ferocious   decent   hateful   mean   unpleasant

4. lion   leopard   jaguar   panther   gorilla

5. sweat sock   sandal   slipper   sneaker   flip-flop

6. highway   turnpike   vehicle   main road   driveway

7. joyous   gloomy   merry   gleeful   happy

8. nephew   grandfather   niece   uncle   brother

9. beautiful   pretty   attractive   lovely   dreadful

10. serious   playful   frisky   active   fun-loving

More I'm Through! What Can I Do? Grade 5 © 2008 Creative Teaching Press

Name: _____   Date: _____

Odd Word Out #2

In each row, all of the words have something in common except one. Find and circle the word that doesn't belong in each group.

1. twirl   spin   twist   whirl   lift

2. comical   funny   amusing   somber   silly

3. confused   thoughtful   bewildered   perplexed   baffled

4. beagle   spaniel   tabby   poodle   bloodhound

5. frightening   dreadful   horrible   terrifying   inspiring

6. ordinary   unusual   strange   weird   uncommon

7. curious   nosy   private   snoopy   inquisitive

8. dandelion   marigold   maple   petunia   violet

9. dangerous   harmful   risky   secure   hazardous

10. trumpet   saxophone   tuba   trombone   guitar

More I'm Through! What Can I Do? Grade 5 © 2008 Creative Teaching Press

What's Missing?

Look at each series of words below. Figure out what the pattern is and add a word that continues the pattern. Then, explain why your word is correct.

Example:

act, big, cot, den, _____**elf**_____

Why? _____The next word must be a 3-letter word that begins with **e**._____

1. a, ad, art, area, _____

   Why? _____

2. able, belt, cars, dime, _____

   Why? _____

3. lot, mat, nip, oar, _____

   Why? _____

4. dead, eye, fluff, gang, _____

   Why? _____

5. ropes, steer, towns, under, _____

   Why? _____

6. proud, often, nails, mouse, _____

   Why? _____

7. Danny, Eddie, Frank, Garth, _____

   Why? _____

8. Annie, Darla, Grace, Jenny, _____

   Why? _____

Finish Line

The race is over. The winner's shirt is pictured below. Which one is it? Use the clues to cross off one shirt at a time to figure out which shirt the winner wore.

❑ The winner's ID tag has at least one digit that is odd.
❑ The winner's ID tag does not have a vowel.
❑ The winner's ID tag doesn't have two of the same digits.
❑ The number on the winner's ID tag is more than 6 x 4.
❑ The product of the two digits on the winner's ID tag is more than 50.

More I'm Through! What Can I Do? Grade 5 © 2008 Creative Teaching Press

License Plate Mix-Up

You and your friends have just gotten new license plates for your bikes. Use the clues to cross off one plate at a time to figure out which one is yours.

- ❑ The sum of the digits on your license plate is not 10.
- ❑ Your license plate has a 7 on it.
- ❑ The sum of the digits on your license plate is more than 20.
- ❑ The number on your license plate is not equal to 1528 + 1231.
- ❑ The sum of the digits on your license plate is not even.

Lost Locker

You have just gotten a new locker. Use the clues to cross off one locker at a time to figure out which one is yours.

- ❑ Your locker number contains a 3.
- ❑ Your locker number has at least one even digit.
- ❑ Your locker number is not equal to 802 x 4.
- ❑ The sum of the first two digits on your locker number is greater than the sum of the last two digits.
- ❑ The sum of the digits in your locker number is greater than 15.

| 1124 | 1113 | 5432 | 3208 | 4543 | 1736 |

More I'm Through! What Can I Do? Grade 5 © 2008 Creative Teaching Press

Outdoor Adventures

Each girl needs a certain piece of sports equipment for her favorite pastime. Use the grid below to help you find out who used which item.

Use the following rules:
- When a possible answer is false, place an X in the box.
- When you find a match, draw a black dot in the box.
- Once you place a dot, no one else can have that equipment, so fill the other boxes under that equipment name with Xs.
- Once someone is matched with a certain piece of equipment, fill the rest of her boxes with Xs since she can't have more than one piece of equipment.
- When there is only one empty box remaining in a row or column of Xs, that must be the true answer, so place a black dot there.
- When you are finished, make sure there is one black dot for each girl.

Use these clues **in order**. They will help you complete the chart below.
1. No girl uses equipment that begins with the same letter as her name.
2. Kerry's equipment has the same number of letters as her name.
3. Cassie's equipment is not used in the water.
4. Brianna's equipment does not have wheels.
5. Renee hates to camp.
6. Stephanie uses her equipment when she hikes in the nearby mountains.
7. Brianna practices using her equipment in the pond near her home.

	Canoe	Kayak	Backpack	Roller Blades	Surfboard
Kerry					
Stephanie					
Brianna					
Cassie					
Renee					

Name: _____ Date: _____

Pet Project

Each boy has a different type of pet. Use the grid below to help you find out who has which pet.

Use the following rules:
- When a possible answer is false, place an X in the box.
- When you find a match, draw a black dot in the box.
- Once you place a dot, no one else can have that pet, so fill the other boxes under that pet with Xs.
- Once someone is matched with a pet, fill the rest of his boxes with Xs.
- When there is only one empty box remaining in a row or column of Xs, that must be the true answer, so place a black dot there.
- When you are finished, make sure there is one black dot for each boy.

Use these clues **in order**. They will help you complete the chart below.
1. No boy has a pet that begins with the same letter as his name.
2. Barry's pet has more than two legs.
3. Perry's pet does not have fur.
4. The type of pet that Larry owns has eight letters in its name.
5. Garry's pet is a mammal.
6. Harry's pet is a reptile, but it does not have a shell.

	Lizard	Beagle	Parrot	Goldfish	Hamster	Turtle
Barry						
Garry						
Harry						
Larry						
Perry						
Terry						

More I'm Through! What Can I Do? Grade 5 © 2008 Creative Teaching Press

Who's Who?

Help the school secretary match the students' first and last names. Use the grid below to help you find out who's who.

Use the following rules:
- When a possible answer is false, place an X in the box.
- When you find a match, draw a black dot in the box.
- Once you place a dot, no one can have that name, so fill the other boxes under that name with Xs.
- Once someone is matched with a name, fill the rest of his or her boxes with Xs.
- When there is only one empty box remaining in a row or column of Xs, that must be the true answer, so place a black dot there.
- When you are finished, make sure there is one black dot for each person.

Use these clues **in order**. They will help you complete the chart below.
1. No student's first and last names have the same number of letters.
2. Andrew's last name has fewer letters than his first name.
3. Aaron's last name has more letters than his first name.
4. The person with the longest first name has the shortest last name.
5. One boy's last name has twice as many letters as his first name.
6. Ann's last name has an "m" in it.
7. Aaron's first and last names have the same number of syllables.
8. Allison's last name is longer than Andrew's.

	Arp	Abel	Adams	Abbott	Abraham	Anderson
Ann						
Alex						
Aaron						
Andrew						
Allison						
Adelaide						

Token Logic #1

Cut out the 9 tokens. Use the clues below to help place the tokens in the correct squares on the grid. A token **may** touch another token on the left, right, top, or bottom, but **not** diagonally. After reading all clues, you may have a token left over. Assume it fits in the last empty box. When you are finished, check to make sure all 6 clues are still true!

Clues

- The ☯ tokens are in the center column, but they do not touch.
- The ★ token touches both ☯ tokens.
- The ☼ token is on the bottom row, but not on the right.
- The ☺ token is on the right side, but it does not touch either ☯.
- The ☾ tokens are in different rows and they each touch a different ☯ token.
- The ⧊ token does not touch either ☾ token.

More I'm Through! What Can I Do? Grade 5 © 2008 Creative Teaching Press

Token Logic #2

Cut out the 9 tokens. Use the clues below to help place the tokens in the correct squares on the grid. A token **may** touch another token on the left, right, top, or bottom, but **not** diagonally. After reading all clues, you may have a token left over. Assume it fits in the last empty box. When you are finished, check to make sure all 5 clues are still true!

Clues

- The ⊙ tokens are on the left, but they do not touch.
- One of the ☺ tokens is between the two ⊙ tokens.
- The ☯ token is in the center column, but it doesn't touch either of the ⊙ tokens.
- Only one of the ▲ is in the bottom row, but it touches the other ▲ token.
- One of the ☾ is on the right column and one is in the center column, but they do not touch.

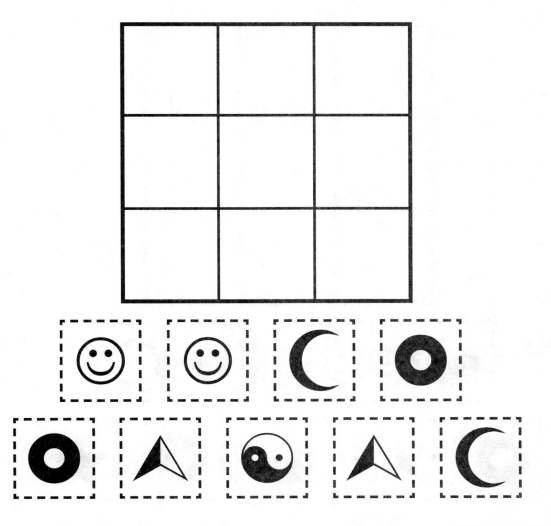

Token Logic #3

Cut out the 9 tokens. Use the clues below to help place the tokens in the correct squares on the grid. A token **may** touch another token on the left, right, top, or bottom, but **not** diagonally. After reading all clues, you may have a token left over. Assume it fits in the last empty box. When you are finished, check to make sure all 5 clues are still true!

Clues

- The ⬆ tokens are in the middle row, but they do not touch.
- The ☼ touches both of the ⬤ tokens.
- Both ⬆ tokens touch the ☼ token.
- The ★ is to the right of the ⬆, but not in the top row.
- The ☯ tokens are not in the same row, nor the same column.

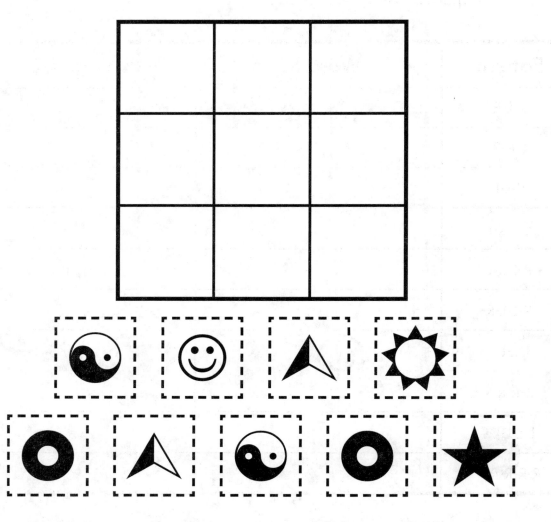

More I'm Through! What Can I Do? Grade 5 © 2008 Creative Teaching Press

Name: _____ Date: _____

Left, Right, Left

The shaded keys on the keyboard below are keys that are typed with the left hand. Unshaded keys are typed with the right hand. Come up with two words that follow each pattern given. A letter may be used more than once per word, but no proper nouns.

Example: R-R-L ➤ *pot, hid, mob, lug, mix*

L = left   Q W E R T Y U I O P / A S D F G H J K L / Z X C V B N M   **R = right**

	Pattern	Word #1	Word #2
1.	R-L-R		
2.	L-R-R		
3.	R-L-L		
4.	L-R-R-L		
5.	R-L-R-L		
6.	R-L-L-R		
7.	L-L-L-L		
8.	R-R-R-R		
9.	L-L-L-L-L		
10.	R-R-R-R-R		

More I'm Through! What Can I Do? Grade 5 © 2008 Creative Teaching Press

Following Directions **57**

Keyboard Puzzler

Each row on the keyboard below has a different value, as shown in the key. Find two words that have the required number of letters and point values to complete the chart. Proper nouns are okay, and a letter may be used more than once per word.

Example: 4 letters and 7 points ⟶ *sand, Chad, bags, fang, hack*

	# Letters	# Points	Word #1	Word #2
1.	3	5		
2.	3	6		
3.	3	9		
4.	4	6		
5.	4	8		
6.	4	10		
7.	4	12		
8.	5	10		
9.	5	12		
10.	5	15		

Key

⬜ = 3 points

⬛ = 2 points

▢ = 1 point

More I'm Through! What Can I Do? Grade 5 © 2008 Creative Teaching Press

Letter Machine

Each letter in the letter machine has been given a value. A = 1, B = 2, and so on. Think of a word that fits each set of clues below. Proper nouns are okay, and a letter may be used more than once per word.

Example: 2-letter word worth more than 20 ➡ by (b + y = 2 + 25 = 27)

A1	B2	C3	D4	E5	F6
G7	H8	I9	J10	K11	L12
M13	N14	O15	P16	Q17	R18
S19	T20	U21	V22	W23	X24
Y25	Z26				

	# of Letters	Point Value	Word
1.	2	less than 10	
2.	2	11–20	
3.	2	more than 20	
4.	3	less than 15	
5.	3	20–30	
6.	3	more than 30	
7.	4	11–20	
8.	4	more than 40	
9.	5	less than 30	
10.	5	40–50	
11.	5	more than 50	

Tricky Letters & Numbers

Each letter in the letter machine has been given a value. A = 1, B = 2, and so on. Think of a word that fits each clue below. A letter may be used more than once per word. Proper nouns are okay. You must use letters from all rows shown for each question. Add up the points for each letter to get a total value for each word.

Example: 4-letter word made from the letters in row 3
Possible Answers: *prom* (value = 62) or *moon* (value = 57) or *room* (value = 61)

Row 1	A1	B2	C3	D4	E5	F6
Row 2	G7	H8	I9	J10	K11	L12
Row 3	M13	N14	O15	P16	Q17	R18
Row 4	S19	T20	U21	V22	W23	X24
Row 5	Y25	Z26				

	# Letters	Row(s)	Word	Value
1.	3	1		
2.	4	2		
3.	4	1		
4.	4	1 & 2		
5.	4	1 & 3		
6.	4	2 & 3		
7.	4	3 & 4		
8.	5	1 & 3		
9.	5	1 & 4		
10.	5	1 & 2 & 3		

More I'm Through! What Can I Do? Grade 5 © 2008 Creative Teaching Press

I've Got Your Number

The keys below represent the keys on a typical phone pad. Come up with two words that include letters from each of the keys given. Each word must have 4 or more letters. A letter may be used more than once. You must use each key shown when making a word. No proper nouns.

Example: keys 5 & 6 ➝ *monk, look*

	Keys	Word #1	Word #2
1.	2 & 3		
2.	3 & 6		
3.	4 & 7		
4.	7 & 8		
5.	2 & 6		
6.	6 & 7		
7.	2 & 4 & 6		
8.	2 & 3 & 8		
9.	2 & 3 & 6		
10.	3 & 6 & 9		

Color Pattern

Follow the key below to complete this design.

1. yellow = prime numbers
2. blue = multiples of 7

3. green = multiples of 6
4. red = multiples of 10

Note: Spaces with no number remain white.

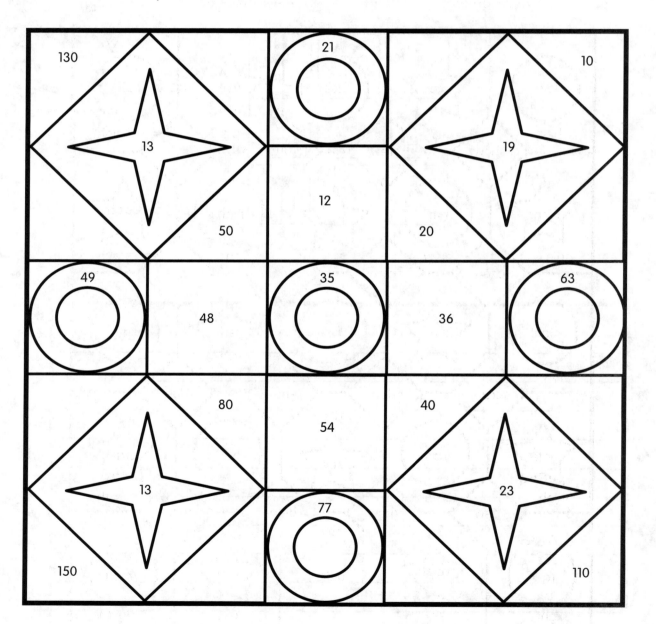

More I'm Through! What Can I Do? Grade 5 © 2008 Creative Teaching Press

Color and Solve

To complete this design, color the words according to the colors specified for their rhyming words in the following key:

1. go = red
2. my = blue
3. you = green

4. bite = yellow
5. late = purple
6. me = orange

Channel Surfing

Use alphabetical order to help figure out which channel number has been assigned to each of the 12 new channels on your local public broadcasting system. Write the number of each channel beneath its picture on the following page.

1. If **antelope** comes before **anteater** in the dictionary, write the number 2 for the "All Music, All the Time" channel. If not, write a 10.

2. If **underwear** comes before **underwater**, write the number 3 for the "Hobby Shopping" channel. If not, write a 6.

3. If **algebra** comes before **alligator**, write the number 9 for the "Nothing But Pets" channel. If not, write a 7.

4. If **fable** comes before **fabulous**, write the number 5 for the "What's Cookin'?" channel. If not, write a 12.

5. If **matrimony** comes after **marigold**, write the number 2 for the "Racing Channel." If not, write a 6.

6. If **rectangle** comes before **rectangular**, write the number 12 for the "Outdoor Network." If not, write an 11.

7. If **mysterious** comes before **mystical**, write the number 8 for the "Babies Only" channel. If not, write a 3.

8. If **cabinet** comes after **cabin,** write the number 7 for the "Home Repair" channel. If not, write a 1.

9. If **balance** comes before **balloon**, write the number 11 for the "Homework Help" channel. If not, write a 6.

10. If **crayfish** comes before **crayon**, write the number 3 for the "Costume Shopping" channel. If not, write a 7.

11. If **computer** comes before **computation**, write the number 4 for the "Mystery Channel." If not, write a 1.

12. If **ornament** comes after **ornate**, write the number 6 for the "Garden Network." If not, write a 4.

More I'm Through! What Can I Do? Grade 5 © 2008 Creative Teaching Press

Channel Surfing

Garden Network

Nothing But Pets

Costume Shopping

What's Cookin'?

Racing Channel

All Music, All the Time

Babies Only

Homework Help

Mystery Channel

Home Repair

Hobby Shopping

Outdoor Network

Get in Shape

Use the numbers and shapes in the Venn diagram on the next page to help answer each question.

1. I am the largest number that lies inside the circle but in no other shapes. _____

2. I am the only number that lies inside the pentagon, the circle, and the square. _____

3. I am the sum of all the numbers that lie inside the hexagon. _____

4. I am the product of the two smallest numbers inside the circle. _____

5. I am the difference between the largest number inside the hexagon and the smallest number inside the triangle. _____

6. I am the sum of the numbers that lie inside both the pentagon and the square. _____

7. I am the only number inside both the circle and the pentagon but in no other shapes. _____

8. I am the only number inside both the triangle and the hexagon but in no other shapes. _____

9. I am the sum of the numbers that lie inside the circle but in no other shapes. _____

10. I am the only number that lies inside the triangle, the pentagon, and the hexagon. _____

11. I am the product of the two largest numbers inside the pentagon. _____

12. I am the only number that lies inside both the triangle and the pentagon but in no other shape. _____

More I'm Through! What Can I Do? Grade 5 © 2008 Creative Teaching Press

Get in Shape

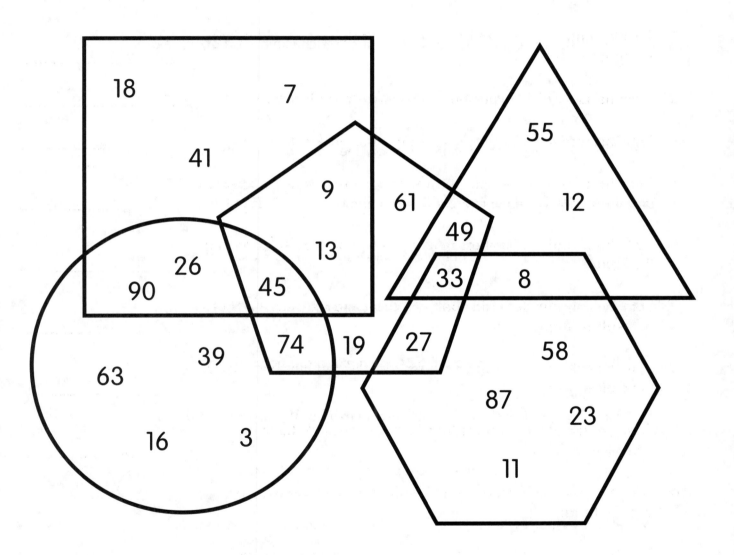

Who's Who at the Zoo?

Solve the math problems to help figure out which number belongs on each animal's exhibit at the new zoo. Write the correct number on the line below each animal on the following page.

1. If 355 + 115 = 460, write the number 8 below the flamingo exhibit. If not, write a 10.

2. If 26 x 18 = 468, write the number 4 below the ostrich exhibit. If not, write a 5.

3. If 456 – 238 = 208, write the number 7 below the zebra exhibit. If not, write a 6.

4. If 369 + 97 = 456, write the number 9 below the polar bear exhibit. If not, write a 12.

5. If 11 x 29 = 319, write the number 5 below the lion exhibit. If not, write a 1.

6. If 287 + 196 = 493, write the number 6 below the monkey exhibit. If not, write a 9.

7. If 871 – 458 = 393, write the number 2 below the panda exhibit. If not, write a 1.

8. If 16 x 15 = 240, write a 7 below the penguin exhibit. If not, write a 9.

9. If 24 x 12 = 268, write a 10 below the giraffe exhibit. If not, write an 8.

10. If 147 x 3 = 441, write a 3 below the hippo exhibit. If not, write a 12.

11. If 299 + 187 = 466, write an 11 below the tiger exhibit. If not, write a 2.

12. If 26 x 14 = 344, write a 1 below the rhino exhibit. If not, write an 11.

More I'm Through! What Can I Do? Grade 5 © 2008 Creative Teaching Press

Who's Who at the Zoo?

_____   _____   _____

_____   _____   _____

_____   _____   _____

_____   _____   _____

Crazy Quilt

Follow these directions to complete the "Crazy Quilt" on page 71.

1. In the upper left-hand box, draw a 5-pointed star and color it red. In the upper right-hand box, draw a 5-pointed star and color it orange.

2. In the lower right-hand box, draw a 5-pointed star and color it purple. In the lower left-hand box, draw a 5-pointed star and color it blue.

3. In the middle box in the top and bottom rows, draw a happy face and color it yellow.

4. Draw and color a yellow sun in the box below the orange star and the box below the red star. Draw and color a yellow sun in the box above the purple star and the box above the blue star.

5. In the 2nd row, draw a big black X in the box just below the happy face. In the 5th row, draw a big black X in the box just above the happy face.

6. In the boxes to the left and the right of each black X, draw and color a brown square.

7. In the 3rd row, draw and color a green triangle in the boxes just below each brown square.

8. In the top row, put a black arrow pointing up in each of the remaining empty boxes.

9. In the bottom row, put a black arrow pointing down in each of the remaining empty boxes.

10. In the 3rd row, draw a red heart in each of the remaining empty boxes.

11. In the empty row that is left, print your initials in the center box.

12. In the boxes on each side of your initials, draw and color a light blue crescent moon.

13. In each of the last two empty boxes, draw and color a black diamond.

More I'm Through! What Can I Do? Grade 5 © 2008 Creative Teaching Press

Name: _____   Date: _____

Crazy Quilt

<table>
<tr><td></td><td></td><td></td><td></td><td></td></tr>
<tr><td></td><td></td><td></td><td></td><td></td></tr>
<tr><td></td><td></td><td></td><td></td><td></td></tr>
<tr><td></td><td></td><td></td><td></td><td></td></tr>
<tr><td></td><td></td><td></td><td></td><td></td></tr>
<tr><td></td><td></td><td></td><td></td><td></td></tr>
</table>

More I'm Through! What Can I Do? Grade 5 © 2008 Creative Teaching Press

Name: _____   Date: _____

Make a Monster

Use colored pencils to color in the grid by following these directions:

1. In rows 12 and 17, color boxes A, B, L, and M brown and the rest of the boxes orange.

2. In rows 5 and 9, color boxes E, F, G, H, and I green.

3. In rows 1, 2, and 3, color boxes E, F, G, H, and I black.

4. In rows 21, 22, 23, 24, 25, 26, 27, and 28, color boxes D, E, F, H, I, and J blue.

5. In rows 10 and 11, color boxes F, G, and H green.

6. In rows 29 and 30, color boxes C, D, E, F, H, I, J, and K black.

7. In row 20, color boxes C, D, E, F, G, H, I, J, and K orange.

8. In rows 13 and 16, color boxes A, B, L, and M brown; boxes C, D, E, F, H, I, J, and K orange; and box G black.

9. In row 18, color boxes A, B, L, and M yellow; and boxes C, D, E, F, G, H, I, J, and K orange.

10. In row 4, color boxes C, D, E, F, G, H, I, J, and K black.

11. In rows 14 and 15, color boxes A, B, L, and M brown; boxes C, D, E, F, G, H and K orange; and boxes I and J black.

12. In row 7, color boxes D, E, F, G, H, I, and J green.

13. In row 6, color boxes D, E, G, I, and J green; and boxes F and H blue.

14. In row 19, color boxes A, B, L, and M yellow; box G black; and boxes C, D, E, F, H, I, J, and K orange.

15. In row 8, color boxes E and I green; and color boxes F, G, and H red.

	A	B	C	D	E	F	G	H	I	J	K	L	M
1													
2													
3													
4													
5													
6													
7													
8													
9													
10													
11													
12													
13													
14													
15													
16													
17													
18													
19													
20													
21													
22													
23													
24													
25													
26													
27													
28													
29													
30													

More I'm Through! What Can I Do? Grade 5 © 2008 Creative Teaching Press

Name: _____   Date: _____

Draw a Dragon

Follow these steps to draw a dragon.

1.

Draw the body as shown.

2.

Add the fins.

3.

Add the tail, legs, and flames.

4.

Draw the rest of the details.

Draw your finished dragon here. Add background details and color.

Name: _____   Date: _____

Draw a Race Car

Follow these steps to draw a race car.

1. Draw the body as shown.	**2.** Add the wheels.
3.  Add the tail fin and the driver.	**4.**  Draw the rest of the details.

Draw your finished car here. Add background details and color.

More I'm Through! What Can I Do? Grade 5 © 2008 Creative Teaching Press

Name: _____   Date: _____

Draw a Stegosaurus

Follow these steps to draw a stegosaurus.

1.
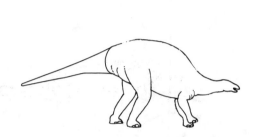
Draw the body as shown.

2.

Add the plates on its back.

3.

Add the eye and the tail spikes.

4.

Draw the rest of the details.

Draw your finished stegosaurus here. Add background details and color.

Finish a Frog

Use the artwork provided below as a guide to help you complete the frog. Color your completed picture.

More I'm Through! What Can I Do? Grade 5 © 2008 Creative Teaching Press

Build a Butterfly

Use the artwork provided below as a guide to help you complete the butterfly. Color your completed picture.

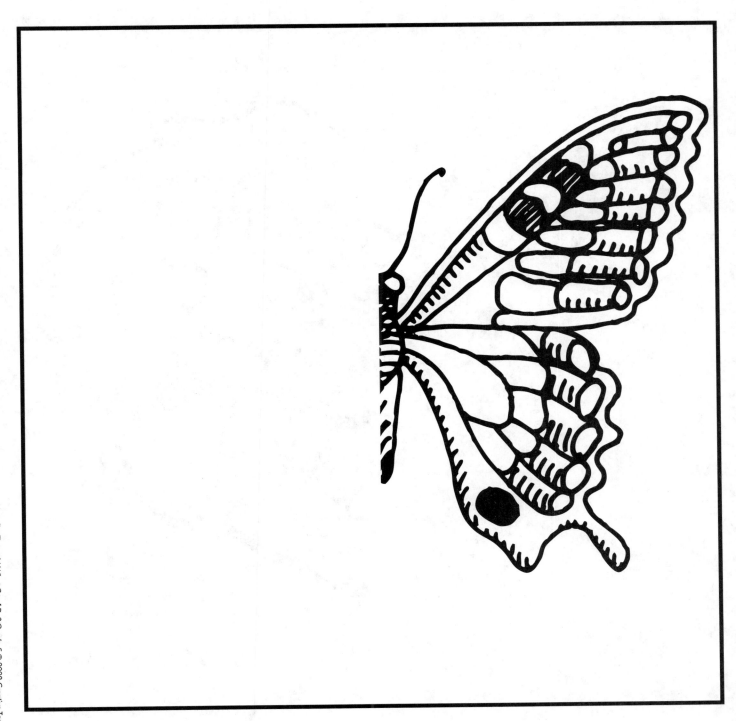

Name: _____ Date: _____

Create a Lion

Use the artwork provided below as a guide to help you complete the lion. Color your completed picture.

More I'm Through! What Can I Do? Grade 5 © 2008 Creative Teaching Press

Design a T-Shirt

Design a T-shirt featuring your own original artwork. Draw in the details and color them in.

Name: _____   Date: _____

Personal Crest

Design your own personal crest. Draw a picture, symbol, or slogan in each of the four sections to show four things that are important to you. Color your finished crest. Print your name in one banner and the year in the other.

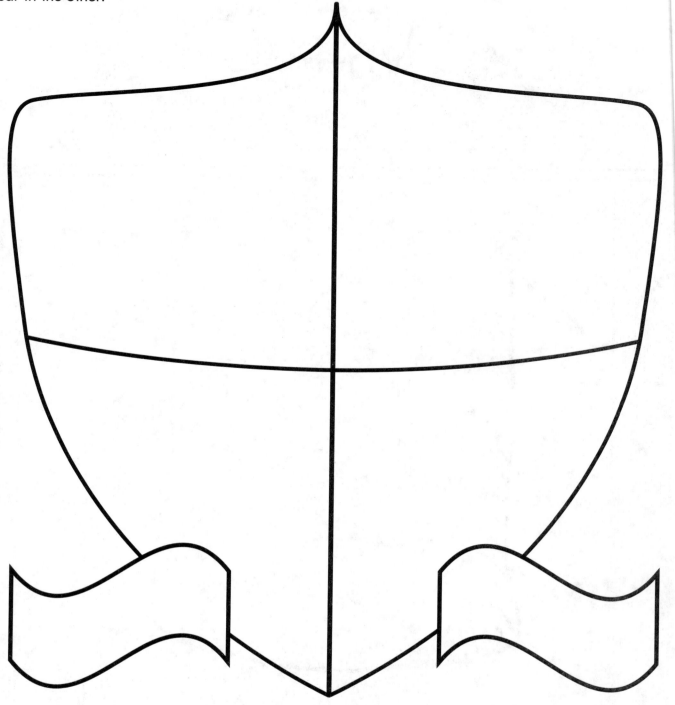

More I'm Through! What Can I Do? Grade 5 © 2008 Creative Teaching Press

Design a CD Case

Design an original CD case. You can even make yourself the star! Draw, color, and add fancy lettering.

Name: _____

Date: _____

Create Comic Strips #1

Design original comic strips. Create and name your characters. Think of problems for the main character, and draw scenes in the boxes below. Be creative!

Create Comic Strips #2

Design original comic strips. Create and name your characters. Think of problems for the main character, and draw scenes in the boxes below. Be creative!

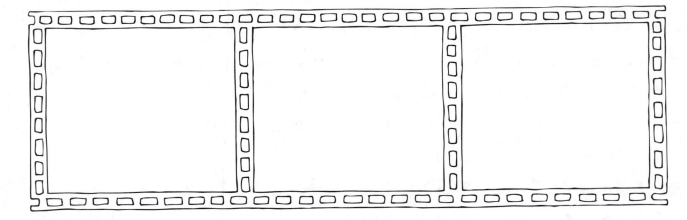

Grid Picture #1

Using a ruler and the grid below, draw straight lines to connect the grid points below in the order given. The first lines have been drawn for you.

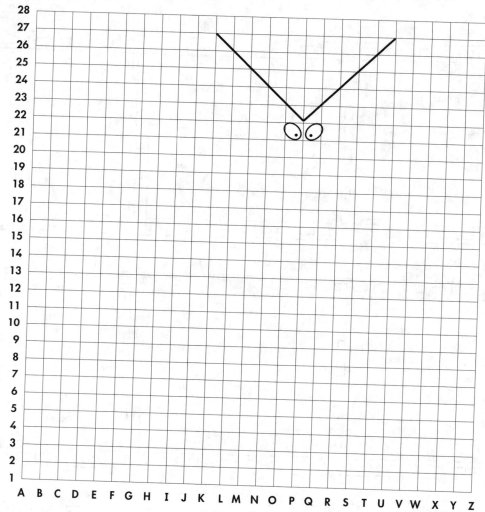

→ K–27, P–22, U–27

→ N–22, R–22, P–19, N–22

→ O–19, Q–19, Q–13, O–13, O–19

→ O–13, M–14, C–14, G–12, M–12, O–13

→ E–13, B–13, E–10, M–10, Q–13

→ D–18, C–19, F–23, J–18, O–18

→ Q–18, V–18, V–24, Y–19, X–18

→ F–23, H–19, J–18, N–17, O–18

→ Q–18, R–17, V–18, W–19, V–24

→ M–10, E–12, B–2

→ M–10, G–16, G–2

→ M–10, S–12, U–2

→ M10, U–16, Y–2

More I'm Through! What Can I Do? Grade 5 © 2008 Creative Teaching Press

Grid Picture #2

Using a ruler and the grid below, draw straight lines to connect the grid points in the order given.

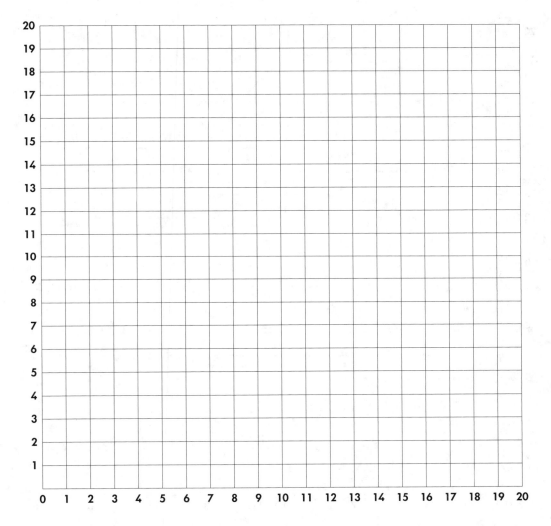

→ (12, 3) (13, 2) (6, 2) (7, 3) (1, 7) (1, 13) (6, 18) (5, 19) (15, 19) (14, 18) (19, 13) (19, 7) (12, 3) (7, 3)

→ (5, 10) (7, 12) (10, 13) (11, 13) (13, 12) (15, 11) (17, 14) (17, 12) (16, 10) (17, 8) (17, 6) (15, 9) (13, 8) (11, 7) (10, 7) (7, 8) (8, 9) (6, 9) (5, 10)

→ (3, 15) (5, 16) (6, 15) (8, 16) (11, 15) (13, 16) (15, 15) (16, 16)

→ (10, 13) (12, 15) (12, 14) (14, 14) (13, 13) (13, 12)

→ (7, 10) (7, 11) (8, 11) (7, 10)

Grid Picture #3

Using a ruler and the grid below, draw straight lines to connect the grid points in the order given.

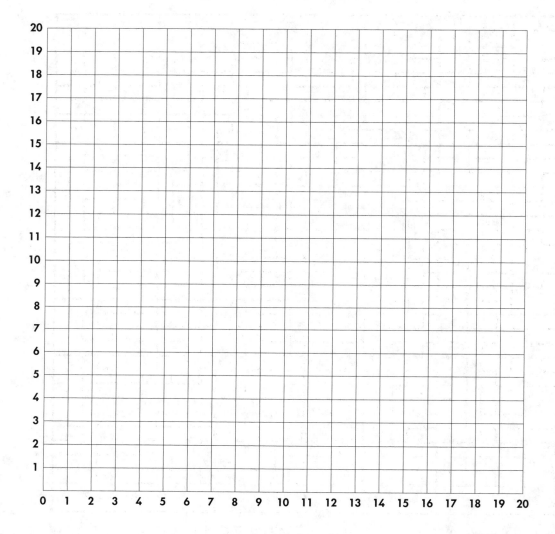

→ (3, 2) (3, 3) (5, 5) (6, 12) (7, 13) (9, 14) (9, 15) (8, 16) (6, 15) (5, 13) (5, 12) (2, 12) (2, 14) (3, 15) (3, 19) (7, 19) (8, 20) (12, 20) (13, 19) (17, 19) (17, 15) (18, 14) (18, 12) (15, 12) (15, 13) (14, 15) (12, 16) (11, 15) (11, 14) (13, 13) (14, 12) (15, 5) (17, 3) (17, 2) (13, 1) (7, 1) (3, 2)

→ (11, 1) (11, 3) (10, 4) (10, 6) (9, 7) (9, 10)

→ (9, 16) (8, 18)

→ (11, 16) (12, 18)

More I'm Through! What Can I Do? Grade 5 © 2008 Creative Teaching Press

Find the Treasure

Start

Finish!

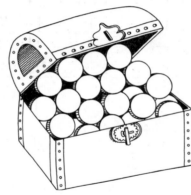

More I'm Through! What Can I Do? Grade 5 © 2008 Creative Teaching Press

Name: _____ Date: _____

Reach the Top

Start

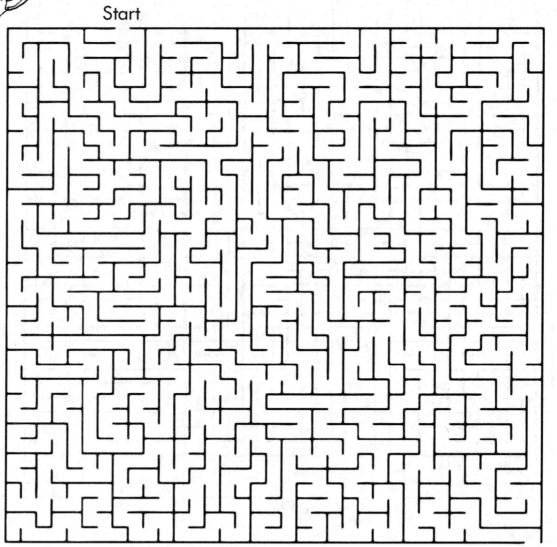

Finish!

More I'm Through! What Can I Do? Grade 5 © 2008 Creative Teaching Press

Collect Your Coins

Start

Finish!

Hive Sweet Hive

Start

Finish!

More I'm Through! What Can I Do? Grade 5 © 2008 Creative Teaching Press

Answer Key

Word Maker #1 (Page 5)
Possible answers include:

aide	pin
ail	rice
aims	ripen
caper	steer
cares	stem
creep	term
crest	tier
mean	treats
other	tress

Word Maker #2 (Page 6)
Possible answers include:

bend	scant
builder	sobs
bunt	sock
cone	stub
cost	taps
done	tinder
past	want
pints	windy
red	wonder

Word Maker #3 (Page 7)
Possible answers include:

arose	rote
art	sewn
dart	tinder
dinner	torn
faint	torte
matter	totes
new	water
pines	wind
rend	wires

Word Maker #4 (Page 8)
Possible answers include:

anger	lies
angles	notary
bit	poor
brisk	pour
city	risk
flies	send
gale	sunken
genes	toys
gnat	tries

Triplets (Page 9)
Possible answers include:

1. tar
2. sit
3. bet
4. tab
5. are
6. sea
7. bit
8. met
9. bat
10. eat
11. ate
12. era
13. tea
14. set
15. sat
16. mar
17. rim
18. ram
19. ear
20. arm

Juggling Vowels (Page 10)
Possible answers include:

soul, soil, seal, sail,
fool, foul, feel, foal, fail
loon, loan, lean, lion
peer, pear, pour, pair, poor
mean, moan, moon
deed, dead, died
tear, tier, tour

Rhyme Time (Page 11)
Possible answers include:

1. snore & store
2. roast & toast
3. moans & tones
4. dream & steam
5. these & trees
6. smart & start
7. share & snare
8. smear & steer
9. smash & trash
10. shade & trade

Fill 'er Up (Page 12)
Possible answers include:

p___t → paint, pellet, print, plant, parrot, point, pocket, priest, pamphlet

t___t → ticket, throat, trout, thicket, thought, tenant, talent, tablet, tryout

d___r → digger, despair, doctor, dipper, diameter, deliver, donor, drummer, divisor, danger

s___d → stood, steed, stayed, scooted, shaped, screwed, salad, strand, scaffold, spend

Code Breaker #1 (Page 13)
A nail in a horseshoe.

Code Breaker #2 (Page 14)
Because it is too far to walk.

Code Breaker #3 (Page 15)
Time to get a new fence.

Skateboarding Fun (Page 16)
Possible answers include:

3-letter words:
boa, sat, bad, rob, fin, bin, get, fat, not, eat

4-letter words:
fate, boar, take, date, sofa, barn, beat, boat, bask, drab

5-letter words:
broad, roads, dates, frost, forks, sting, steak, darts, break, funds

6 or more letters:
skater, boards, brakes, breaks, fortune, sturgeon, surfing, frosting, forest

Rock Climbing Adventure (Page 17)
Possible answers include:

3-letter words:
tin, ink, kin, kit, mob, tan, ten, rib, got, cub

4-letter words:
term, ring, grim, vent, germ, mint, grin, vote, tick, cork

5-letter words:
trick, climb, curve, cover, cured, nerve, never, evict, truck, given

6 or more letters:
crumble, tricking, buckle, blocked, combined, climbed, mockingbird, becoming, convertible, verdict

State Stumper Crossword (Page 18)

Across	Down
5. New York	1. Virginia
6. Oregon	2. Georgia
7. Alaska	3. Kansas
8. California	4. Vermont
11. Florida	9. Indiana
	10. Maine

Spelling Stumper Crossword (Page 19)

Across	Down
3. butterfly	1. gerbil
5. shrimp	2. elephant
8. rattlesnake	3. buffalo
10. donkey	4. parakeet
11. dragonfly	6. hamster
	7. camel
	9. turkey

Weather Word Search (Page 20)

```
W E A R T E H R T H U S Q S S U I Z F O T
O T S O R F F L I E R S U N A B I S T D
N O M O S O R L O O U T Q O F L C A R R
L I H N T G O Y M B D N I M C L A W E O
R A I L F I B L I Z S N O Q U A T S U U
N A I N B M I T O R Z Z D R O U L L C G
R A V L E R N O O S N O M U Q L H A H
H U R R I C A N E C M O N S O S L E E T
M O O P Z L A S O T J Y G I L Q T A U C
E N T E Z R T A I O N M E L N U T T T O
N C L C A M I T O R H A F I O P W W E E
I O A K R T D U A L L P N G C S R A L F
O I U L D E E L L O I N Y H I Z E V U I
P N Q M Q N L O D A N R O T A T Z E V M
E Y U O N H W A O Z Z R I N R E T O P E
R T Z I E G P W O L B B M I E D E T Y F
W R A P A P V E L F R E D N U H T C F R
A R I E L Z E S F O R T N G R E E T Y M
S C L E A N M E R C T B W X Q U I O P Z
Q U A L T Y E R W D E I O P L R A I H N
```

Get a Job Word Search (Page 21)

```
P L A N D A R C H P O L R E T R O P E R
O S O L D A S T R O N A U T A S T L I N
L O T E C H N I C I A N M E N C V H I E
I X E R T Y L C R U I G H S T R E E S W
T E A T L A W Y E R W E Y R P U M N B E
I C T R W C A T R S E B M U L P X E O P
C E Y E E M S P T O D O C N T Y R N L O
I U U L A I T U I T E J Q U E A S A T G
A I H P T N G H U C R U M E R E T I R W
N P J R H T D O C O X D Z E R Q I C E E
H L A E E S M E T D L G A S U M C I H A
I A C P F L S C A N A E M I E C K R P T
U R E A T E A C H E R K K C L A I T A P
R E R C C D W L O V S A H R A H P C R B
K E T S W O I J S E I A W A L M E E G E
L O N U D O M T T E R N T T E K I R L O P T
B I I N L A R C H I T E C T E C S E T I
R G A A I N H O C K R A M E L H T P O L
E N S L P R E T N E P R A C L E E A H O
N E Q U E T S I G O L O E A H C R A P T
```

Word Chain #1 (Page 22)

Answers will vary.

Word Chain #2 (Page 23)

Answers will vary.

Addition Pathways (Page 24)

Top → 1 + 10 + 11 + 5 + 16 + 40 + 14 + 8 = 105

Middle → 2 + 8 + 12 + 3 + 13 + 21 + 16 + 14 = 89

Bottom → 5 + 6 + 17 + 27 + 3 + 31 + 4 + 8 = 101

Subtraction Pathways (Page 25)

Top → 100 − 24 − 16 − 2 − 17 − 12 − 15 − 13 = 1

Middle → 99 − 8 − 20 − 12 − 29 − 11 − 10 − 4 = 5

Bottom → 101 − 3 − 5 − 33 − 21 − 9 − 15 − 13 = 2

What's the Sum? (Page 26)

1. 400 + 119 = 519
2. 333 + 199 = 532
3. 356 + 207 = 563
4. 700 + 444 = 1,144
5. 902 + 599 = 1,501
6. 775 + 377 = 1,152
7. 654 + 389 = 1,043
8. 603 + 199 = 802

What's the Difference? (Page 27)

1. 700 − 287 = 413
2. 399 − 111 = 288
3. 200 − 179 = 21
4. 300 − 155 = 145
5. 800 − 672 = 128
6. 600 − 299 = 301
7. 400 − 333 = 67
8. 900 − 666 = 234

Tricky Subtraction (Page 28)

1. 211 − 176 = 35
2. 674 − 107 = 567
3. 896 − 409 = 487
4. 765 − 299 = 466
5. 391 − 255 = 136
6. 301 − 153 = 148
7. 864 − 211 = 653
8. 964 − 466 = 498

Math Mysteries (Page 29)

1. SUBTRACT 957 − 386 = 571
2. ADD 843 + 659 = 1,502
3. MULTIPLY 966 × 40 = 38,640
4. DIVIDE 975 ÷ 13 = 75
5. ADD 188 + 966 = 1,154
6. MULTIPLY 30 × 54 = 1,620

Math Path #1 (Page 30)
End: 1,113

Math Path #2 (Page 31)

1. 270
2. 1,240
3. 954
4. 1,888
5. 2,509

Number Puzzle #1 (Page 32)

1. 9 + 41 + 18 + 27 + 11 + 8 + 68 = 182
2. 68 × 65 = 4,420
3. 87 × 70 = 6,090
4. Circle: 9 + 41 + 18 + 27 + 11 + 8 + 68 +15 + 65 = 262
   Pentagon: 15 + 65 + 87 + 70 = 237
   Difference: 262 − 237 = 25
5. Square has a sum of 146
6. 52 × 87 = 4,524

Number Puzzle #2 (Page 33)

1. 37
2. 12
3. 30
4. 13
5. 10
6. 15
7. 7
8. 77
9. 64
10. 55

It All Adds Up #1 (Page 34)

5	1	2	4	3	6
3	4	6	5	2	1
6	2	3	1	4	5
4	5	1	2	6	3
1	6	4	3	5	2
2	3	5	6	1	4

It All Adds Up #2 (Page 35)

2	1	3	4	5	6
3	5	2	6	1	4
4	6	5	1	2	3
1	2	4	3	6	5
6	3	1	5	4	2
5	4	6	2	3	1

It All Adds Up #3 (Page 36)

4	6	5	2	1	3
5	1	6	3	2	4
3	2	1	4	5	6
2	3	4	5	6	1
6	4	2	1	3	5
1	5	3	6	4	2

It All Adds Up #4 (Page 37)

4	2	3	1	5	6
1	6	4	5	3	2
5	3	2	6	4	1
6	4	5	2	1	3
3	1	6	4	2	5
2	5	1	6	4	2

It All Adds Up #5 (Page 38)

7	2	4	1	8	5	6	3	9
1	6	5	9	3	4	7	2	8
9	8	3	2	6	7	1	5	4
5	4	2	6	7	8	9	1	3
3	1	9	5	2	9	4	8	6
8	9	6	4	1	3	2	7	5
2	3	1	8	4	6	5	9	7
4	5	8	7	9	2	3	6	1
6	7	9	3	5	1	8	4	2

It All Adds Up #6 (Page 39)

1	9	6	5	8	7	4	2	3
7	4	8	2	6	3	9	1	5
3	2	5	1	4	9	8	6	7
6	3	4	7	9	8	1	5	2
9	1	7	6	5	2	3	8	4
5	8	2	4	3	1	7	9	6
8	5	1	3	2	4	6	7	9
4	6	9	8	7	5	2	3	1
2	7	3	9	1	6	5	4	8

It All Adds Up #7 (Page 40)

8	1	2	4	7	6	3	9	5
6	7	4	5	9	3	1	2	8
5	3	9	2	1	8	6	7	4
3	9	5	8	2	1	7	4	6
1	2	8	6	4	7	9	5	3
7	4	6	3	5	9	2	8	1
4	6	7	9	3	5	8	1	2
9	5	3	1	8	2	4	6	7
2	8	1	7	6	4	5	3	9

It All Adds Up #8 (Page 41)

6	5	3	4	2	1	7	8	9
4	8	9	3	7	5	6	1	2
1	7	2	6	9	8	4	5	3
7	2	4	5	8	9	1	3	6
9	1	6	7	3	2	8	4	5
8	3	5	1	4	6	2	9	7
2	6	1	8	5	3	9	7	4
5	4	8	9	6	7	3	2	1
3	9	7	2	1	4	5	6	8

What a Pickle! (Page 42)

1. 987 − 457 = 530
2. 987 + 985 + 984 + 978 = 3,934
3. 984 − 457 = 527
4. 98 + 97 + 95 + 94 + 89 = 473
5. 9,875 − 4,578 = 5,297

I'm Puzzled (Page 43)

1. 9,764 − 3,467 = 6,297
2. 9,764 + 9,763 + 9,674 + 9,673 = 38,874
3. 9,763 − 3,476 = 6,287
4. 976 + 974 + 973 + 967 + 964 = 4,854
5. 97,643 − 34,679 = 62,964

B-I-N-G-O! (Page 44)

Row Totals:

R1 = 187   R2 = 193   R3 = 156
R4 = 204   R5 = 185

Column Totals:

B = 45   I = 113   N = 155
G = 269   O = 343

Questions:

1. 48   3. 298
2. 158   4. 48

Odd Word Out #1 (Page 45)

1. bunch
2. minor
3. decent
4. gorilla
5. sweat sock
6. vehicle
7. gloomy
8. niece
9. dreadful
10. serious

Odd Word Out #2 (Page 46)

1. lift
2. somber
3. thoughtful
4. tabby
5. inspiring
6. ordinary
7. private
8. maple
9. secure
10. guitar

What's Missing? (Page 47)

1. Any 5-letter word that begins with "a" (atlas, arrow, apple, allow, ashes).
2. Any 4-letter word that begins with "e" (each, eggs, earn).
3. Any 3-letter word that begins with "p" (pop, pan, pit).
4. Any word that begins and ends with "h" (hush, hunch, harsh).
5. Any 5-letter word that begins with "v" (vault, voice, veins).
6. Any 5-letter word that begins with "l" (llama, lions, large).
7. Any 5-letter boy's name that begins with "H" (Harry, Henry, Heath).
8. Any 5-letter girl's name that begins with "M" (Marcy, Maria, Marla).

Finish Line (Page 48)

Winner's ID Tag is DX-97

License Plate Mix-Up (Page 49)

License plate number is 4791

Lost Locker (Page 50)

Locker number is 4543

Outdoor Adventures (Page 51)

Kerry—canoe
Stephanie—backpack
Brianna—kayak
Cassie—roller blades
Renee—surfboard

Pet Project (Page 52)

Barry—hamster
Garry—beagle
Harry—lizard
Larry—goldfish
Perry—turtle
Terry—parrot

Who's Who? (Page 53)

Ann Abraham
Alex Anderson
Aaron Abbott
Andrew Abel
Allison Adams
Adelaide Arp

Token Logic #1 (Page 54)

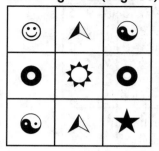

Token Logic #2 (Page 55)

Token Logic #3 (Page 56)

Left, Right, Left (Page 57)

Possible answers include:

1. pen, pry, key, lap, ham
2. dip, won, boy, zoo, run
3. new, yes, her, jab, mad
4. food, gold, toot, rope, boot
5. melt, kept, lake, prow, melt
6. lash, lean, keep, oral, heel
7. drew, base, feat, acre, tree
8. holy, honk, loon, milk, join
9. trees, crews, feast, greet, rests
10. milky, hilly, loopy, jumpy, onion

Keyboard Puzzler (Page 58)

Possible answers include:

1. Ben, cob, bin, lab, fan
2. gas, bar, tan, dim, pan
3. ewe, try, toy, put, Poe
4. calm, band, bang, cans, clan
5. lags, glad, sash, fads, dash
6. goat, dart, lift, lots, date
7. were, tree, poet, port, quit
8. blade, clasp, sandy, thank, baggy
9. crate, crews, wreck, trend, scope
10. putty, worry, quiet, route, error

Letter Machine (Page 59)

Possible answers include:

1. be, ad, ha, Ed
2. me, he, Al, am, as
3. oh, to, by, so, us, ox
4. bee, ace, fed, cab, Abe
5. him, kid, odd, doe, dip
6. moo, pot, Ron, sow, let
7. dead, deed, fade, cage, beef
8. rows, moon, poem, toys, exam
9. faced, blade, faded
10. games, green, liked, plane, spade
11. quiet, zebra, study, pound, wrote

Tricky Letters & Numbers (Page 60)

Possible answers include:

1. cab, bad, fad, fed, ace
2. high, hill, Jill, kill
3. deaf, bead, fade, face, beef
4. cage, hide, like, file, flag
5. mane, dome, Rome, foam, pear
6. ring, pork, pink, roll, pool
7. tons, post, port, rots, most
8. raced, cream, named, brace
9. beast, feast, steed, waste, state
10. range, joker, pearl, flame, hoped

I've Got Your Number (Page 61)

Possible answers include:

1. beef, fade, deaf
2. mend, mode, defend
3. rigs, sigh, pigs, ship, sprig
4. rust, trust, ruts, puts, purrs
5. moan, coma, comma, bacon, common
6. mops, prom, room, moons, soon
7. bang, coin, hang, chin, main
8. fate, cute, beet, beat, cuffed
9. fame, foamed, moaned, made, mean
10. women, wooden, oxen, moody

Color Pattern (Page 62)

yellow: 13, 19, 23
blue: 21, 35, 49, 63, 77
green: 12, 36, 54, 48
red: 10, 20, 40, 50, 80, 110, 130, 150

Color and Solve #2 (Page 63)

Red: low, hello, doe, hoe, flow, tow, toe, dough, show, row, snow, whoa

Blue: fly, pie, die, rye, high, pry, thigh, why, buy, sigh, sky, guy

Green: show, brew, through, glue, chew, screw, canoe, flu, crew, due, renew, blue, pew, grew, drew who

Yellow: white, fright, knight, polite, night, fight, write, light, tight, kite, slight, unite, excite

Purple: ate, wait, eight, weight, gate, crate, freight, trait

Orange: flee, knee, tea, key

Channel Surfing (Pages 64–65)

Garden Network—Channel 4
Nothing But Pets—Channel 9
Costume Shopping—Channel 3
What's Cookin'?—Channel 5
Racing Channel—Channel 2
All Music, All the Time—Channel 10
Babies Only—Channel 8
Homework Help—Channel 11
Mystery Channel—Channel 1
Home Repair—Channel 7
Hobby Shopping—Channel 6
Outdoor Network—Channel 12

Get in Shape (Pages 66–67)

1. 63
2. 45
3. 247
4. 48
5. 79
6. 67
7. 74
8. 8
9. 121
10. 33
11. 4,514
12. 49

Who's Who at the Zoo? (Pages 68–69)

Giraffe—Exhibit 8
Panda—Exhibit 1
Lion—Exhibit 5
Zebra—Exhibit 6
Flamingo—Exhibit 10
Tiger—Exhibit 2
Hippos—Exhibit 3
Monkey—Exhibit 9
Penguin—Exhibit 7
Polar Bear—Exhibit 12
Ostrich—Exhibit 4
Rhinoceras—Exhibit 11

Crazy Quilt (Pages 70–71)

Row 1: red star, black arrow pointing up, yellow happy face, black arrow pointing up, orange star

Row 2: yellow sun, brown square, black X, brown square, yellow sun

Row 3: red heart, green triangle, red heart, green triangle, red heart

Row 4: black diamond, light blue crescent moon, initials, light blue crescent moon, black diamond

Row 5: same as row 2

Row 6: blue star, black arrow pointing down, yellow happy face, black arrow pointing down, purple star

Make a Monster (Page 72)

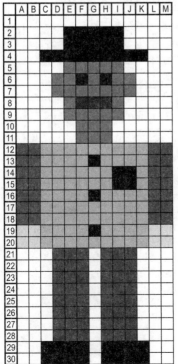

Draw a Dragon (Page 73)

Drawing should look similar to picture in box 4 but with background details.

Draw a Race Car (Page 74)

Drawing should look similar to picture in box 4 but with background details.

Draw a Stegosaurus (Page 75)

Drawing should look similar to picture in box 4 but with background details.

Finish a Frog (Page 76)

Left-hand drawing should look similar to right half of page.

Build a Butterfly (Page 77)

Left-hand drawing should look similar to right half of page.

Create a Lion (Page 78)

Left-hand drawing should look similar to right half of page.

Design a T-Shirt (Page 79)

Individual student drawings will vary.

Personal Crest (Page 80)

Individual student drawings will vary.

Design a CD Case (Page 81)

Individual student drawings will vary.

Create Comic Strips #1 (Page 82)

Individual student drawings will vary.

Create Comic Strips #2 (Page 83)

Individual student drawings will vary.

Grid Picture #1 (Page 84)

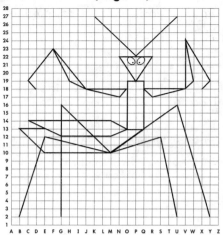

Find the Treasure (Page 87)

Hive Sweet Hive (Page 90)

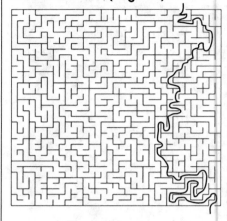

Grid Picture #2 (Page 85)

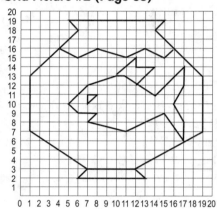

Reach the Top (Page 88)

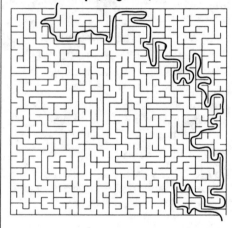

Grid Picture #3 (Page 86)

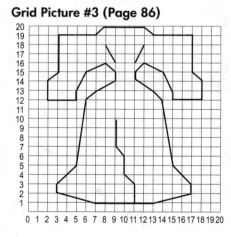

Collect Your Coins (Page 89)

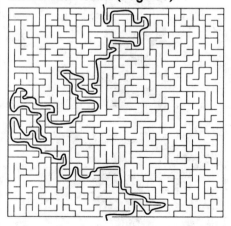